GUIDES

MINECRAFT: MMORPG

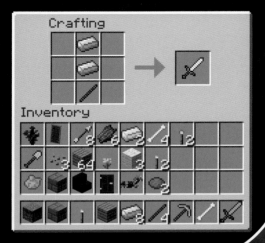

CHERRY LAKE PUBLISHING • ANN ARBOR, MICHIGAN

by Josh Gregory

Published in the United States of America by Cherry Lake Publishing
Ann Arbor, Michigan
www.cherrylakepublishing.com

Reading Adviser: Marla Conn, Read With Me Now
Photo Credits: Cover and page 4, ©Phil's Mommy/Shutterstock; page 6,
©Maskot/Getty Images; page 10, ©Syda Productions/Shutterstock; page 14,
©Joe Scarnici/Stringer/Getty Images; page 15, ©makar6809/Shutterstock;
page 16, ©Niferure/Shutterstock; all other images by Josh Gregory

Library of Congress Cataloging-in-Publication Data has been filed and is available
at catalog.loc.gov

Cherry Lake Publishing would like to acknowledge the work of the Partnership
for 21st Century Learning. Please visit *www.p21.org* for more information.

Printed in the United States of America
Corporate Graphics

21st **Century Skills** INNOVATION LIBRARY

Contents

Chapter 1

Exploring New Worlds

Minecraft is a truly massive game. No matter how much you play, there is always something new to do. There is better gear to **craft** for your character. There are new places to explore and

Every time you start up a new game of *Minecraft*, you're in for a completely different experience from the last time.

Playing together with friends in multiplayer mode is one of the best parts of *Minecraft*.

new things to build. And if you think you've run out of things to do, you can start a brand-new game with a whole different world to explore.

One of the most fun ways to play *Minecraft* is to meet up with friends online for multiplayer adventures. In most versions of the game, up to eight players can meet online to explore, build, and battle together. *Minecraft*'s built-in multiplayer mode has provided countless hours of exciting adventures to the game's millions of players around the world. But what if there was a way to play with more than just a few players at once? Can you imagine a version of *Minecraft* that isn't just multiplayer, but *massively* multiplayer? Believe it or not, such a thing already exists!

From the very beginning, *Minecraft* has always been a game about creativity. Players get to build and reshape the game's world in almost any way they can imagine. Some highly talented players take their creativity outside the boundaries of the game. They have programmed many additions and changes to the

Minecraft has always had a strong following among computer programmers and game designers.

Making Changes

Minecraft is constantly growing and changing. Since the game's first version was released in 2009, its creators have regularly released updates for players to download. Some updates simply fix bugs or add support for newer computer **hardware**. But others make major changes to the game. Most of the features that are now a core part of the *Minecraft* experience were not originally in the game. These include weapons such as bows and arrows, enemies such as creepers, and even multiplayer mode.

Sometimes modders played a role in bringing these important features to *Minecraft*. Today, horses are a common element of the main *Minecraft* game. But they were originally created as a mod. The game's developers saw how popular the mod was and how well it worked. They asked its creator to help them make horses an official part of *Minecraft*.

main *Minecraft* game. Then they put their creations online for other players to download. These unofficial updates to the game are known as **mods**.

Mods played a big part in *Minecraft*'s growing popularity during the game's early days. The same kinds of players who were drawn to a game about building things were even more interested. They realized the potential for adding their own unique twists to the game. As word of *Minecraft*'s amazing possibilities for mods spread around the world, a huge community of modders grew online. They shared ideas for new projects and programming tips with one another.

Since the first version of *Minecraft* was released in 2009, thousands of different mods have been shared online. There are mods that increase the game's difficulty and mods that change the appearance of different objects in the game. Other mods add new types of enemies, building materials, or objects. One popular mod adds massive dinosaurs to the game. Another

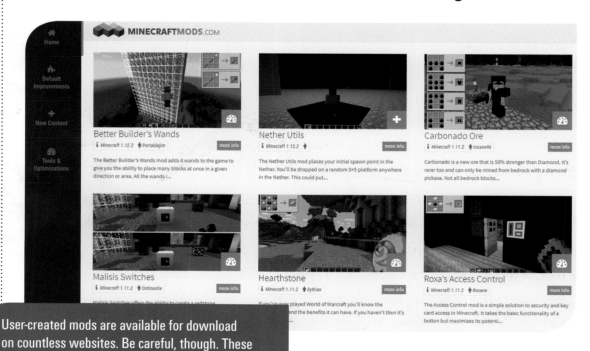

User-created mods are available for download on countless websites. Be careful, though. These downloads are not officially supported by Mojang.

lets players use real programmable computers within the world of the game.

The most amazing mods completely change the way *Minecraft* is played. There are mods that place your *Minecraft* character into a sticky situation, such as being stuck on an island in the sky or a vast desert with few supplies. They make you think creatively to find a way out. There are also mods that turn *Minecraft* into a puzzle game. But perhaps the most amazing mods of all are the ones that turn *Minecraft* into a massively multiplayer online role-playing game, or MMORPG.

MMORPGs are far beyond anything you've seen in regular *Minecraft* multiplayer. Hundreds of players can join together to go on adventures. You can also forget everything you thought you knew about playing *Minecraft*. Some of the most popular MMORPG mods change almost every aspect of the game, from how you earn new equipment to how you explore the world. Are you ready to give it a try?

Chapter 2

Massively Multiplayer

MMORPGs might seem like the kind of game that could only exist with the latest technology. But they have actually been around for much longer than you might think. People have been joining up online to explore fantasy worlds since the early

Massively multiplayer online games are a great way to meet up with friends online.

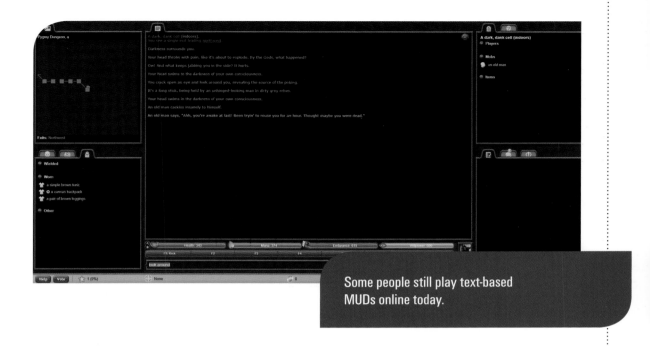

Some people still play text-based MUDs online today.

days of personal computers and the internet. In the 1970s, computer programmers began creating online games called multiuser dungeons, or MUDs. MUDs did not have the incredible graphics and huge worlds that players are used to today. In fact, most of them were little more than text displayed on the screen. The words players saw would describe their surroundings and what was happening around them. The players would enter text commands to say what their in-game characters would do next.

The first modern MMORPGs were released in the late 1990s. *Ultima Online* (1997) and *EverQuest* (1999) drew hundreds of thousands of players into MMORPGs

Ultima Online might look simple compared to modern games, but it was groundbreaking in the 1990s.

for the first time. Unlike MUDs, these games had colorful graphics, sound effects, music, and everything else you would expect in a modern video game.

Today, MMORPGs are among the most popular and successful types of video games available. There are many different ones for players to choose from. By far, the most popular example of the **genre** is *World of Warcraft*. You may have even played this game. More than 100 million players around the world have created accounts on the game. And even though the

Most of the earliest MUDs were not created by big game companies. Like *Minecraft*, they were created by game fans who had their own unique ideas. They used their programming skills and creativity to design and build online worlds for other players to explore.

Like *Minecraft*, many modern MMORPGs have also become favorites of the modding community. After they get tired of the world in their favorite games, some modders try building new areas for players to explore. Other modders do the opposite. After an MMORPG has been running for many years, the game's developers have probably made many changes to it. So some modders create versions of their favorite MMORPGs that are more similar to the way the games were when they first came out.

game was released in 2004, it continues to have millions of players today.

In modern MMORPGs, huge numbers of players can explore the same game world at the same time. They can join together to go on all kinds of adventures in a variety of settings. For example, *World of Warcraft* takes place in a fantasy world where dragons, knights, and magic are all common. Other MMORPGs take place in futuristic science-fiction worlds or in realistic settings that are much like the world we live in. There are even MMORPGs set in the worlds of popular franchises such as *Star Wars* and *The Lord of the Rings*.

Players try out the latest version of *World of Warcraft* at a game convention in Germany.

In most MMORPGs, players spend much of their time battling monsters, completing **quests**, and searching for rare items. They can explore sprawling wilderness areas or make their way through dangerous **dungeons**. They can also challenge each other to **duels** to prove their combat skills. When they aren't fighting, they can craft items, go shopping, wander through huge cities, or simply hang out with other players.

Because MMORPGs are based on teamwork or competition with other players, communication is a big part of most games. As they explore, battle enemies, and search for loot, players talk with each other using text or voice chat systems. Many players form groups called **guilds**. Guild members often meet up at scheduled times to go on adventures in their favorite MMORPGs. They share weapons, armor, and other gear to help make each other's in-game characters stronger. Experienced members might also share game tips with newer players to help them get the hang of playing.

Many MMORPG players use headset microphones to talk to other players during game sessions.

It takes more than just a big world full of players to make a true MMORPG. After all, MMORPGs are not only massively multiplayer and online. They are also role-playing games. So what is a role-playing game? It is a game where you take on the role of a character and guide that character through a lifetime of adventures. Along the way, your character will grow more and more powerful. For example, in most role-playing games, your character will earn something called

The first role-playing video games were based on "pen and paper" role-playing games such as Dungeons and Dragons.

experience points by completing quests or defeating enemies. Earning enough experience points will allow your character to gain a level. This improves the character's abilities. Another major way of gaining power in most role-playing games is to find new weapons, armor, and other gear.

Every role-playing game has its own unique systems for building up your characters. Some are fairly simple, while others are incredibly complex. But the main idea is always the same. As your character becomes more powerful, you can fight stronger enemies, visit more dangerous areas, and take on more advanced quests. The fun of the game comes partially from trying to reach the most advanced areas of the game, defeat the toughest enemies, and find the best gear.

Not all role-playing games are massively multiplayer or even multiplayer at all. And not all massively multiplayer games are role-playing games. But when both genres are combined, the result is something truly special. Can you believe that it's possible to play this kind of game inside *Minecraft*? All you need to do is find the right mod to use.

Chapter 3

Getting Started

So how exactly can you set out on your own *Minecraft* MMORPG adventure? Start by picking which one you want to try. The most popular *Minecraft* MMORPG out there is called Wynncraft. Other well-known options include Avalon and Falling Kingdom. There are many others, too, but the most popular ones are more likely to have lots of players online at any given time. They are also more likely to stay running for a long time.

Wynncraft offers a detailed world to explore.

Adding an MMORPG server to your multiplayer server list only takes a few clicks.

To join one of these games, you will need the original PC version of *Minecraft*. Console versions do not allow players to join **servers**, so they will not work with these kinds of user-made mods.

Each MMORPG has its own unique server address. For example, the address for Wynncraft is *play.wynncraft.com*. To find other MMORPG servers, search online or talk to friends who play *Minecraft*. These games are usually shared among friends and online communities. They are not advertised widely or available in stores.

Coming and Going

Because *Minecraft* MMORPGs are free projects made by fans, you might run into some problems with them that you don't see when playing regular *Minecraft*. For example, you might come across bugs that cause the game to stop working correctly. You might also notice that the controls are not quite as smooth as they normally are.

The biggest potential problem is that privately created *Minecraft* servers are not guaranteed to last. You might spend weeks building up a character in an MMORPG, only to find out one day that the server is no longer up and running. All your progress is lost! You might also hear about a cool new *Minecraft* MMORPG from a friend, only to find that it no longer exists by the time you try to play it. This goes for the MMORPG servers mentioned in this book, as well. But even as your favorite servers disappear, new *Minecraft* MMORPGs are being created, so you'll always have something to play.

Start *Minecraft*, then choose the "Multiplayer" option from the main menu. Now click the Add Server button. Enter the address of the MMORPG you want to join under "Server Address." In the "Server Name" section, simply type a name to remind you which MMORPG you are joining. *Minecraft* will remember the name and put it in your list of servers, so you can go back to it anytime.

Click Done and you will now see the MMORPG server on your list of multiplayer servers. Double-click it to join the game. You will soon find yourself in the MMORPG world you chose. It's that simple!

Try moving around and exploring a little bit. Depending on which MMORPG you decided to play, the screen might look almost exactly like it does in a regular *Minecraft* game. Or it might be something completely different. Familiar objects from *Minecraft* might do things that are completely different from what you're used to. Each MMORPG server has its own features and ways to play. It will always take some getting used to when you start a new one.

Unlike in a regular game of *Minecraft*, you start off with plenty of weapons in Avalon.

For example, when you join the Wynncraft server, you'll find yourself holding a compass and looking at a purple gate in the distance. Nearby, there are some words floating in the air. If you read them, you will get some helpful hints for how to play the game. Most major *Minecraft* MMORPG servers include these kinds of **tutorials** to help new players.

If you try to activate the compass in your character's hand, a menu will pop up on the screen. It offers the chance to choose which "world" you would like to

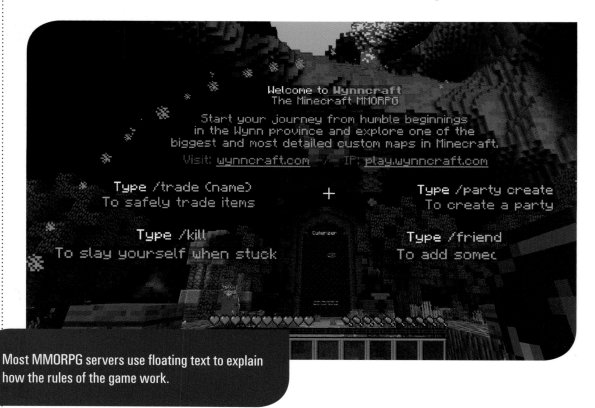

Most MMORPG servers use floating text to explain how the rules of the game work.

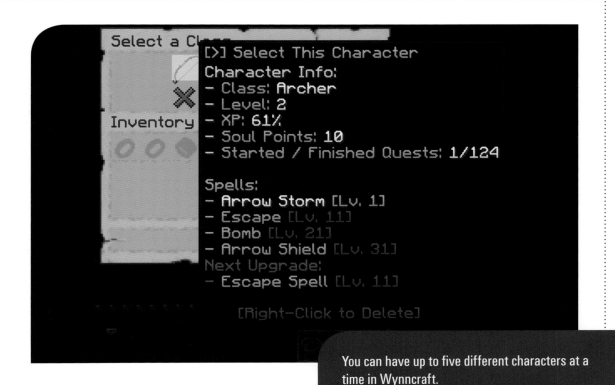

Select a Cl

[>] Select This Character
Character Info:
- Class: Archer
- Level: 2
- XP: 61%
- Soul Points: 10
- Started / Finished Quests: 1/124

Spells:
- Arrow Storm [Lv. 1]
- Escape [Lv. 11]
- Bomb [Lv. 21]
- Arrow Shield [Lv. 31]
Next Upgrade:
- Escape Spell [Lv. 11]

[Right-Click to Delete]

Inventory

You can have up to five different characters at a time in Wynncraft.

join. Each one is exactly the same. A Wynncraft world can hold up to 75 players at a time, so choose one that has room for you.

Now you will have the chance to create a character. Start by picking a class. This is a category that determines which kinds of weapons and abilities your character will have. An archer specializes in bows and arrows. A warrior uses powerful **melee** attacks. Mages use magic spells. Finally, assassins are fast-moving characters that specialize in sneak attacks. Pick whichever one sounds the most fun.

You'll talk to many NPCs as part of your MMORPG adventures.

Now it's time to start exploring and gaining experience. You'll find yourself in the game's first area. Right-click on the nearby character to get your first quest. This is a non-player character, or NPC. NPCs are computer-controlled characters within the game. They will give you quests and sell you items. You will also see other characters running around. Each one has a unique name floating above its head. These are player characters. They are controlled by other players, just like you.

Your first quest will send you out to explore the nearby area. You'll be able to fight animals, monsters, and other enemies. Each one you defeat will give you experience points. Collect enough experience points and you will level up. Your main goal in the game will be to keep leveling up and getting stronger so you can explore more dangerous areas of the game.

MMORPG servers have one major difference from regular *Minecraft* that you'll probably notice right away. You can't mine or build anything! However, MMORPGs usually have other features to make up for this. For example, the combat is often more interesting than it is in regular *Minecraft*. Instead of simply clicking on enemies over and over and swinging your sword, you might be able to use a wide variety of other combat abilities. In Wynncraft, for example, you can click your mouse buttons in different combinations to cast spells.

While this is just a description of one specific MMORPG server, most of them will follow the same basic structure. You will join up and read through a few tutorials. Then you can start questing and leveling up. Along the way, you'll meet many other players with the same goals.

Chapter 4

Staying Safe Online

Anytime you play a massively multiplayer online game, you will probably be interacting with other players. After all, that's one of the main reasons to play this kind of game. Sometimes you might play with a group of friends you already know in real life. But even then, you will probably find yourself

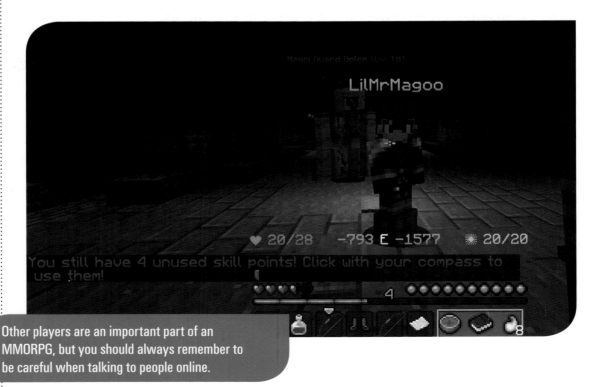

Other players are an important part of an MMORPG, but you should always remember to be careful when talking to people online.

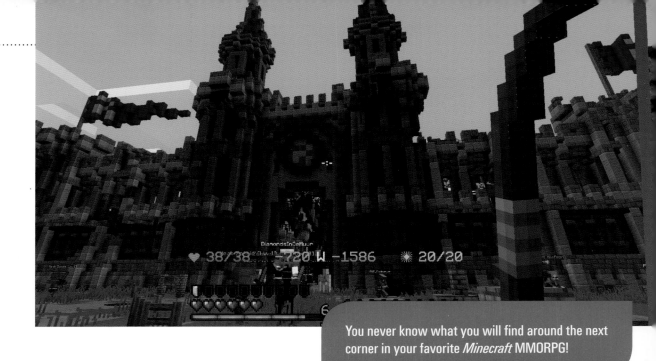

You never know what you will find around the next corner in your favorite *Minecraft* MMORPG!

playing alongside strangers from time to time. This isn't necessarily a bad thing. Most people online just want to enjoy the game the same way you are. And some MMORPG players have even formed lasting friendships with fellow guild members.

Even though most MMORPG players are probably not bad people, you still need to be very careful anytime you play a game online. It is no different than any other internet activity. There is always a chance that the stranger you're playing a game with is trying to hurt you or cause trouble for you. This means you always need to follow online safety rules, even if your fellow players seem friendly and helpful.

Ask Before You Play

Be sure to get permission from a parent or teacher before you start playing *Minecraft* online. They might have specific rules they would like you to follow when you play online games. Also, if they know you are playing an online game, they might be able to help you avoid sharing information about your identity by mistake.

Always do your best to protect your identity. You don't want strangers online to know your name, where you live, or anything else about you. Don't put your real name or any other clues about who you are in your *Minecraft* screen name. Don't reveal this information in the game's text chat window, either. You should even avoid sharing this kind of information when playing with friends you know in real life. If strangers are in the game world with you, they will also be able to see the messages you type.

Your name is just one of many things you should avoid revealing online. Don't talk about your hometown, the name of your school, or the names of people you know in real life. Avoid mentioning the details of your daily schedule. Someone who wanted to hurt you could use this information to find where you are.

If someone tries to send you computer files or asks you to send files, tell them no. You should also turn down any requests to become friends on social media, exchange emails, or send photos to each other. Be careful when clicking on any links to websites from strangers.

This all might sound scary. But if you follow the rules, you can have fun with *Minecraft* MMORPGs while staying safe online. Simply play the game and avoid chatting about anything other than the game itself. And remember that if anything online makes you feel weird or uncomfortable, you can quit the game.

It is also important to take regular breaks from your game. It can be easy to lose track of time when you are having fun, but playing too much at once is not good for anyone. If you have other things you need to do, or if a parent is asking you to quit playing, remember that you can always play some more later. Real life is always more important than video games, no matter how cool they are or how many of your friends are playing.

The world of *Minecraft* MMORPGs is waiting for you to start exploring. What kind of adventures will you go on?

Glossary

craft (KRAFT) make or create

duels (DOOLZ) battles between two players in an MMORPG

dungeons (DUHN-jinz) areas in an MMORPG where players can battle enemies and search for treasure

genre (ZHAHN-ruh) a category of creative work

guilds (GILDS) organized groups of players in an MMORPG

hardware (HAHRD-wair) computer equipment

melee (MAY-lay) hand-to-hand combat

mods (MAHDS) user-created modifications to a video game

quests (KWESTS) in MMORPGs, quests are goals for players to complete in exchange for experience points, loot, or other rewards

servers (SUR-vurz) computers shared by two or more users in a network

tutorials (too-TOR-ee-uhlz) explanations and lessons to help new players learn how a video game works

Find Out More

BOOKS

Milton, Stephanie. *Minecraft Combat Handbook*. New York: Scholastic, 2015.

Milton, Stephanie. *Minecraft: Guide to Exploration*. New York: Del Rey, 2017.

WEBSITES

Minecraft
https://minecraft.net/en
At this official *Minecraft* website, you can learn more about the game or download a copy of the PC version.

Minecraft Wiki
https://minecraft.gamepedia.com/Minecraft_Wiki
Minecraft's many fans work together to maintain this detailed guide to the game.

Index

About the Author

Josh Gregory is the author of more than 125 books for kids. He has written about everything from animals to technology to history. A graduate of the University of Missouri–Columbia, he currently lives in Chicago, Illinois.